The Really King of September

Moshumee T. Dewoo

Langaa Research & Publishing CIG
Mankon, Bamenda

Publisher:

Langaa RPCIG
Langaa Research & Publishing Common Initiative Group
P.O. Box 902 Mankon
Bamenda
North West Region
Cameroon
Langaagrp@gmail.com
www.langaa-rpcig.net

Distributed in and outside N. America by African Books Collective
orders@africanbookscollective.com
www.africanbookscollective.com

ISBN-10: 9956-552-73-9

ISBN-13: 978-9956-552-73-3

Table of Contents

Preface

This is abuse.

It is all unwanted, of course.

It is highs and lows. It is the mind shaken inside out. It is the heart that fixes it. It is good friends that help through it. It is craving good food and loud music. It is hating this too, on most days. It is calling the doctor because of a bruise and cancelling the appointment with him minutes later. It is a man-child that knows all too well how to gaslight. It is a nightmare in broad daylight. It is dignity destroyed. It is a curse to fight at high price. If you cross paths with a demon, that is all this you will have for a while. You will not run from it. You cannot. Trust me, I have tried. I should not have. Because from there, "Leaving behind nights of terror and fear…I rise, I rise, I rise". Maya said it first.

It is beautiful, isn't it?

Orange Skies

Round
Round
You turn
Round
Bound
To sound
Merry
You
Go
Round
Round
Like a hound
To the pigs
Like a flare
To the sky
Fair
Though
No lamp
Be there
In the night
A prayer
Must
Bare
Beware
It is there
You are there
It is you
It is two
At the door
In your eyes

Like the rides
And the tea
And the ties
That kept me
Like the tree
That left me
Still
Sitting
Standing
Bowed
Waiting
At the roots
Of the early
Oak
Worn
Down
Disavowed
Like a plea
A pea
It was
Like you were

You will be

The Girl without Glue

I hurt
Everywhere
From the hair on my head
To my neck
And my womb
In bloom
In June
Dead tune
My core
Is blue
I scream
Ice cream
No more
It hurts
I hurt
Ice blue
My legs
They shake
I shake
I cry
I hurt
You weigh
Your wait
You loom
In gloom
And groom
And prowl
At the gates
Of whomsoever
You can bite

Into

Bitte?

It is love
You swore
But
No more
Of me
Is left
A pit
Of pity
A desert
Whenever
You leave
Whenever
You come back
Every time
I hurt
Everywhere
You hurt
Everywhere
From my hands and my feet
To my spine
I
Hurt
You
Hurt
Everywhere
All the time

Everywhere

The Two-tongued Healer

A monster
Bewitched
Two-tongued
The switch
Healer
A bitch
Bad
Bright
Kind of kitsch
And bloody
A monster
Some Nietzsche
A toddler
And you
Are
No monster
A martyr
You left her
You pressed me
You felt her
Unbelt me
Unflawed
Pan
Really?
This is nice?
As nice as you can be?
Really?
Liar
Liar
Your pants are overawed

Overused
Honey

The Mother

Your tale
A trick

Polaroid

My body
Breathes
To heaven
The third
Piece
Finally
Makes sense
I make peace
With my wits
Gone to Sheol
For a while
And then back
Without end
With some plumes
I now fly
But I do not
Like you do
Like your monkeys
Like the lost boys
With the lost keys
Do
Yet, I do
Oh! I do
I do now!
Without you
Finally
I am free
I see three
Without glue
With the Book

On my arm
It's a shield
Understand
That
You
And
I
Are like
Peter and Wendy
That
You
Are infant
Ancient
Pure

Debris

Crumbs

Just like you told me

Finally
Finally
How I am
Yes! I am

Me

Finally

Pastures

And I woke up
Short of night
Thinking that it was me
Thinking that it was all because of me
That everything was in ruins because of me
This is what you told me
Didn't you, baby?
Everyday, baby
I cried
Short of life
Feeling that I was not enough
I was nothing
I did not do enough
I did not do anything
I was not pretty enough
I had not been anything
Ever
And I wondered
If I could have done better
If I could have done more
If I could have been more
If I should have allowed more
If I should have let the hook
Get the better of me
One time
Once more
Maybe then…
Maybe you…
Who knows…?
I know

And you know
That it was you
It was you
It was you who did not do enough
It was you who were not enough
It was you who did not give enough
And it was you who gave too much
You did too much
You were too much
You screamed too much
You lied too much
It was too much
It was just too much
Of nothing
Nothing real
Nothing, really
Because you are nothing
Really
And that scared you
Because you knew that I would walk away
Because you knew that I would live past you
If I knew
But I knew
And I knew that you knew
And you knew that I knew
Everything about you
And that scared me
So you screamed even more
And you lied even more
And you did so much more
And you became so much more
Because I stopped believing you
Because I never did

I did not believe your screams
I did not believe your lies
I did not believe your promises
Of green pastures
And sweet goodbyes
Because
Under my feet
Was nothing
Nothing that I had
Nothing that wanted
Nothing for me to suffer
Ever
Since the ninth
Of September

Because

I wanted
To grow
Up

I wanted
To grow
Old

Veiled

It is who you are
It is who I am
It is not what you need
It is not what I want
It is who you are
It is who I am
When I am
Dancing
On the moon
With you
It is who I am
When I run
To the stars
With you
When I live
When I die
When I let go
And I let cry
In the storm
With you
It is who I am
It is what I am
It is what you do not know of
It is what you cannot feel

Love

He will not let you

You see?

Crash

Let me walk
Core on fire
Let me run
Dead desire
Take me back
To land
And augur
Talk me down
To my knees
Arms stretched out
I tire

Let me walk
Take me back
Talk me down

Soft lyre

Secret Place

That morning
In that cold cup of coffee

You lost me

Steady

Two words
I faint

F60.81

Count
Two
One
To
No more
The skill
To pen
The tongue
Slows down
As blood
To death
As flood
To man
To son

Daleth

Christian Life

I've been alive
Way too long
Why don't you
Come
Back
And make
Things
Right
Make me
Rise
Back to stone

My soul
Stuck in bone
I've been in love
With a knife
Way too long
Why don't you
Come
Back
And take me
Right
Back to Köln

My stone awaits
My bones are dry
I've been alive
Way too long

Seconds
Hours
Eons

And
Flesh

And
Gone

Soulmate

Put your dreams on my chest
It's your safe place
Do it one more time
Do it all again

A hundred more times
Multiply by ten
I'll always be there
Multiply by ten

Somehow

I want your chest

Somehow

I want your chest
In my dreams

Somehow

Nervous

20 pages left
Until I finish this book
The last chapter was not fun
The last pages were not mine
I wrote them all over
I re-wrote every line
I wrote myself therein
I wrote myself some more
I wrote myself
A stain
I wrote myself
In pine

I must finish this book…
20 pages left
20 pages
To dine

Italy

The church
White
Fades
Time
From the hill
I watch you swim
In the lake
Dark
Blue
And green
It is summer
I love you
I love your skin
Burning

Later

A shower
Soap in your eyes
I kiss you
On my lips
Some beer
Music
We laugh
You sweat
You snap
I sweat

Later

I lose a bracelet
With the water
My pearls are gone

Later

It is set
I see you
It is done

Later

Swine

In the years
That have passed
Like the rain
You have drowned
A foot
Stool
A fool
A clown
For a crest
My love
Lover
My strife

Mercy!
Mercy!

Please
Leave me

Unfortunate District

Flicker
Flicker
Flicker
The lights are on
Always
On
To
Flicker
Red
Unholy
Hell
Has it broken loose?
Where am I?
Why am I here?

Did I fail a test?

Why did you bring me here?
It is war!
It feels like it
Are we at war?
The women
Are armed
Armoured
Enamoured
It seems
I look closer
You tell me to
It is a farce
You warn me

To wish them well
I do

And they go on
To love on men
Hungry

And we go on
To our den
Hungry

Wait
Hold on

Who the heck are you?

Art

Do I soar
When I hope not?
Do I hope
When I know not?
Do I know
When I see not?
Do I stand
When I feel not?

Do I feel
When I fall not?

Ketchup and Big Trucks

I do this
For the children
And their children
And their children
And their children
The thousands of them
That are to come

Of the rib

Of Zion

Land of Strangers

Eight strikes nine
Until
You brush your teeth
Until
It is bed time
Until
I am alone
Until
You rest
Against
My nature
My role
My potter

My ghoul

You have lost
Control

Bold

When I cut the hair
Of an old woman
Emptied in scold
Because I cared
When I made a dress
For a little girl
Birthday carolled
Because I cared
When I drove for hours
To clothe labour
The devil, behold!
Because I cared
I meant it all
Because I cared
While you carved me out
Because I cared
And tore me cold
Because I cared
And knocked me bold
Because I cared
Because I never lived for myself
Because I cared
Because I did not keep love on a shelf
Because you cared
They all
Were told

Did you?
Did you care?
Did you ever dare?

Cold fire

Brazen
Galaxy
Far
Lost
In my mind
Your mild
Collides
Against my flesh
To make a way
To the eve
Of my past

At last

At last

My half
The other
I slide
I backslide
Purified
I turn
No pride
Like a sunflower
To your colour
To your wild

I spin
Hollow shell
At low tide

I bend
Ordinary

I slip
Untied

Bruin Café

My friends know that my heart is broken
That it broke a lot of times
That I stumbled
And fell
Cross on back
Backward
A lot of times
Already
I should get back up
Yes! I should stand up
One more time
For myself
For others
Just like me

My friends do not know
That my heart broke too many times
That I stumbled
And fell
Cross on back
Backward
Too many times
Already
And I would much rather sit back
Yes! I want to sit back
This time
On myself
On others
Just like me
And consider the heavens

And my friends
And you
Doing nothing
Better

I am changed
Forever

Praise

Mirror
Mirror
On the wall
Tell me
The wisdom
Of the cooing dove
Tell me
Of things to come
And those to starve
Tell me
The Kingdom come
And its grand cove
Tell me
Mirror
Tell me
All things
Tell me
Mirror
Tell me
All things
Tell me
Mirror
Tell me all things

Tell me all things
And those above

Word Salad

Your shirt
Is drenched
As pillow
Over
Sole
Sadness
To hide in Willow
The creek
Runs its course
Rash
To slit reason
Like madness
Holds the balance
Between ache
And roar
And treason
A con
Always in season
Bubble knows
He loathes
The Fall
And the thrill
Of the Darling's kiss
Swept under the rug
And prayed to be forgotten
To thin the herd
Of the Little White Bird

Your shirt, Shepherd
Stands tall

A most tedious service
To us

The routine of monsters
Afterall

Corpse

I swear
I was

Once

King of the Hill

Hail
King of high poise
Hail
Your rituals
Spells
And toys
Hail
Your command
Your grin
And ploys
Hail
Your voice
Deceit
And noise
Hail
King to be saved
King to pardon
King who knows nothing
And much less
What is common
Hail
King of the pot
The plot
And the twist
Hail
King of the lot
And the cat and the dog
That I keep alive
Unshod
Even through the fog

Solid
Hail
King of small things
And odd beginnings
Hail
King of good pose
And whatever that does
Hail
King of hail
Of Hell
And its grail
Hail
The King
The Hog
The Cleanse
Prisons
Fortunes
Snakes
And back ends
Hail
King without hands
King without gowns
King without friends
Dropped in a circus
Of spiders
Worms
Whores
And failures
At forty
All four
Disarmed
All five
As you are

King
On trial
For one crime
Too many
Held in frame
Vain
Blank
A carcass of the time
That stands for a writ
Of habeas corpus
From you
For you
King
Meandering
King of none
King for nothing
King but part-time
King and bluffing

King for a dime
A mime
Huffing
And puffing

Curse

Marred
As the rose
And her petals
Sailing
Up
Stream
You went
When you learnt
That I could turn night
Into day
Light
And live still
To fancy
A pansy
For a trade
Off
A stray
Past the peak of your spring
Past your bloom
Made of wax
Gliding across your years
A rōnin
For hara-kiri
As
Delilah
Cut through the Sun
In collapse
Having eaten
Of the Jerusalem cherry

A pariah
In two Acts

A pariah
Mata Hari

Blindfold

That's no man
My sweet fox
That's a demon

But that's not my problem

I Think I Won

I had hoped to write about you
It would have been a poem…
Something about how much I loved you
Something about how you had changed my life
For the better
Something about setting off into the wild blue yonder
With you
To the Moon and beyond
Kind of thing
Something
About
Grey hair
Wrinkles
A barbecue
A lake
A forest
Children
We would be holding hands
It would have been a poem…
Something about how you had brought me to my knees
Quickly
Something about how I felt at home
With you
You were home
It's true
I thought it was crazy
I was crazy
I would have wanted to take it slow
Because that is who I was
I took things slow

I was slow
Steady
Slow
Steady
Slow
But you had rushed into me
It was a crash of bodies *
All flames
A sacrifice
Suddenly
A shoe that fit
A bit of Cinderella
Upside down
Something out of the blue
Something about rapids and no canoe
So
I had hoped to write about you
It would have been a poem
But I had also thought about that night in the kitchen
When, for the first time
In a long time
I remembered what an empty cage felt like
I was spent
Frozen
You wouldn't stop talking
You wouldn't stop walking
I didn't want you to come nearer
I couldn't bear for you to touch me
I couldn't recall the train ride home
I didn't want to come back
I was afraid
Naked
I had left you

I made sure that you wouldn't know about it
My bags were packed
It made me smile
I hadn't smiled
It had been a year
Then two
And so
I had hoped to write about you
It should have been a poem…
Something about how I had needed you
Wanted you
Wanted you uncoiled
Roped down
The wooden chair
Closer
But you could never say any of these things to me
That I had hoped to write about you
Roped down
The wooden chair

Closer

Restored

The worlds have aligned
To give me back
Gold
Mine
My mind
I will speak it now
From the rooftops
Till sundown
I will tell of those things
That make of me
The talk of the town
I will tape to the walls
And the city glow
Those things
That made you ugly
So
The worlds have aligned
You are just a photo

I noticed just now
Your beer belly and receding hairline
And it looks like the crocodile got a piece of you
So
You are just a photo

Alien

My man
A friend
Little green man
From Mars
With green eyes
And long hair
The one that I imagined
The one made for me
A fiend
Instead
The foe knew first
His gift I got
As I begged
As your skin
My man
Became
Stronghold
Soon to see
Fifty
Yours
Not mine
Immobile
I am thirty
And some
Driving
Passing by the old house
Tidying up
The mess
Of yourself
Along a black mile

Of virtue seeping
Repeating
In me
I lock the doors
For fear of losing myself
The arms of the North open up
I shut the windows
I throw the keys
To the angel of death
That lived in your crust
It wouldn't last
I trusted
Long
Or better it be
The evil that I know
Than an old grin that starts to hold

Anyway
I must go
I am baking bread
It's for my family

My man
What is your name again?

Silent Treatment

Groundfires run deep
Winter is on

Reason breaks in

I think this is Happiness

I didn't think the age to come
When the clouds would wash away
But it came
There
In the overlay
Winked a kind ray
I gave in
I found myself
In the littlest thing
In a warm blanket
Caught in a ring
And a loud tint of clay

I was in Bali
I was in Timbuktu

He had been saving me
A beginning
Quietly forging
Everything new

More than Ever

I gather
That they tried to nail me
After failing each other

Make no mistake
I bowed only to the latter

Wisdom to Hide

Let's drop the whole 'strong women' thing
Let's start talking about wise ones in its place
Because that
That is noteworthy
Because I know that I'm strong
I was knit to be
We all are
All of us, women
Because I am every woman
They are me
And we are strong
It is wise that we are not
Not enough
Not often enough
So we learn it
We get it
Over time
We get it
We lean down to wartime
We get it
We rise from the dead
We get it
We raise children
We get it
We love to abandon
We get it
We fight for our lives
We fight evil boys
We fight for the world
We get it

We get it

We do not pass it around
We watch each other get it
We wait

This is wisdom

We get it

Infant Hope

The kids have set up an army
Of plastic wheels and dinosaurs
The dogs may just have built a mausoleum
For a flock of birds
Feathers
And groans
To trap the cows and the sheep
In buildings made of Legos
Pushed to the sides now
For a gilded reredos
They too must worship something
I suppose
They dig around for treats
And toys
To toss
Like confetti
And tear like cotton
Candy
Someone's started singing
It must be my sister
I can't stop smiling

I can get used to this
Forever after

In-and-Out

It takes a while
To leave behind
What is outgrown
This is not so much
A matter of strength
Than it is pride
Consumed
By the fear
Of failure
And the unknown
But once these cease
To wake us well
The roads show rest
And give bed
For wounds to turn
To timber
To ashes
And coast
Stretching new ground
Until eyes unfurl fresh lens

Then, hearts desire
What I think is soul sense

It's a trance that awaits
That we sit face to face

It's the past in the mist
And memory, unassailed

Bonfire Night

It's an eye for an I
The sort of fracas
Where loss is prize

That Home may Bloom

It has been a year of great endings
I cheer to my second Jeep
My time and that creep
I have wishes to send
I have to pleasure a few
It must be this
The longed-for thing
And a little bit more
That I cannot tell you

Printed in the United States
by Baker & Taylor Publisher Services